PREFACE

While this work is extremely personal and painful to share, after much deliberation I decided that it needed to be made available for consumption.

The world lost a brilliant comedian and actor when the great Robin Williams took his own life in 2014. Two years earlier, a personal hero of mine - former NFL linebacker Junior Seau - did the same. Most people did not understand the tragedies. Robin had life by the proverbial throat, and he was near the top of his game. How could a man so gifted and so accomplished take his own life? And Junior, who I had the pleasure of getting to know while he played for the Miami Dolphins, was much the same. He was an icon. He enjoyed wealth. He was a good looking man. Yet, he took his own life. America - and the world - simply could not understand.

Suicide, you see, is a anomaly. It does not follow a pattern. It cannot be easily explained. And, to those who never experienced the serious thought of it, it cannot be understood.

What follows in this book seeks to help explain the thoughts, the emotions, the feelings, the despair and the simple desire to say forget it. My life has been a living hell, and I think about suicide every day. It is a thought that welcomes me, embraces me, calls to me. In some ways, it's my best and most long-time friend. Yet, I've resisted the allure. Why? I'll explain that.

Unfortunately, I truly believe suicide is an action that can never truly be understood by anyone. I will do my best to explain it, however. I will tell you the signs, from my perspective at least. I will tell you what the thoughts feel like. I will tell you how easy it was to sit with a loaded gun on my lap or a bottle of pills in my hand. Something stopped me. Some would say the thought of saying no and continuing was heroic. I would not agree. But some would say the thought of accepting fate and ending one's life is cowardice. That's where I say bogus.

Understand, I am not advocating suicide. That would be foolhardy and irresponsible. But I am trying to explain why one would choose to take his or her own life.

If you are thinking of it yourself, my words can offer solace. I kept putting it off and putting it off, hoping that I would find one magic solution to take away my suffering. While it didn't quite work that way, I found a reason to live. And I'm still here. Maybe my words will allow you to see the path that is right for you. I hope you choose to live. I have chosen that thus far.

But the true target of this work is not the person contemplating the act. My target is much broader. It is the group of people - family, friends, lovers, etc. - that is left behind when someone they know chooses to take his or her own life. These people are left to wonder why this tragedy happened. They feel bad and often blame themselves. They think there is more they could have done to prevent the action. As a result, they live with guilt and depression themselves. For those people, please do not beat yourselves up. You did not choose this. It happened. And, it probably happened with much thought behind it. You were not abandoned haphazardly. It was painful to leave you behind. If it were not for you, this action would have likely occurred much, much sooner. The reason your loved one lasted as long as they did was because of how they felt about you, and leaving you behind was much more difficult than the final act.

Not to dwell too much on Robin Williams, but he did what he felt he must. As many of those who will read this work can relate to him, I use him in my preface to illustrate my point. While we collectively mourn his loss, we should celebrate Robin's departure. It was a decision he likely struggled with for some time, and it was an action that was harder to do than it was to act in all his illustrious roles combined.

After his death, Junior Seau was diagnosed with chronic traumatic encephalopathy - a brain disease caused by too much head trauma during his years on the football field. This was a free-spirited man, one who enjoyed himself and whose smile stays with me to this day. Junior used to sing a song by Sean Paul in the locker room, and I remember the Dolphins getting Paul to record a message for Seau during a team awards banquet. Junior laughed when it was played, and that singular memory will be how I personally remember him.

But his injuries caused him to think differently than most others, and suicide became his choice. Fans cried and mourned his loss, but they never understood what the man was going through. And that is the crux of this issue.

Let's allow that Robin Williams' and Junior Seau's decisions to end their lives - and the decision of a great many of those who do the same - likely came after much deliberation and was probably the most difficult choice they ever made.

Rest in Peace, Robin and Junior.

And Rest in Peace to everyone else who made the decision to end their lives. I hope they all found the peace they so desperately craved, and I - for one -

celebrate their departure as they made the difficult decision they deemed best for themselves.

ADDENDUM

This manuscript was produced during moments of extreme stress and depression. Many of the thoughts contained within are of a deep and dark nature.

The decision to commit suicide is not one to be taken lightly. There are moments in the work where I decide to take my own life. In fact, numerous chapters contain that idea.

I did not go back through the chapters and make any changes to the content, as that would not be true to the intent. I explain why I did not commit suicide later in the manuscript.

Table of Contents

THE REAL QUESTION

Life or death.

Who really cares?

When you live on, despite overwhelming odds and through immense pain, is it worth the hassle and struggle? Many would say yes. I'm here to tell you the answer is a resounding no.

Death is the ultimate release, the closing act on a tragedy many call life.

Think about it. You are born and struggle to learn how to walk, talk and act. It is a constant process to grow into the person you are to become. As you age, your body begins to break down, along with your mental capacity. Somewhere, the laws of diminishing returns begin to creep in.

That chore, which seemed so ordinary and simple three years ago is now an arduous process, one that consumes your time and your energy merely to complete it.

You discover pains and aches in places you did not even know existed.

You begin to realize life, simply, is not worth the effort.

A promising career, one that presented a life's worth of fulfilled goals, was in the grasp and all but assured. The building blocks for success were laid. The outcome seemed destined. Then, in one quick flash, an instant so fleeting you did not even notice it, everything is changed. A 16-year-old moron runs a stop sign and crashes into your vehicle.

Rather than seek medical attention, the career beckons. Surely, you could get by with one more major assignment while you are out of town, with that treatment only a day or two away.

Years later, you look back and scoff. Why put work above health? What were you thinking? Certainly, work is not going to value or reward your decision. No, instead, your bosses will merely serve to crap upon you while trying to convince you your excrement bath was actually a shower in Evian.

Through constant misdiagnosis, substandard medical procedures and poor medical personnel, a small problem is magnified, turned into a gaping hole the size of the former Twin Towers that once graced the New York City skyline before a group of terror mongering psychos crippled America in a horrific attack that will never be forgotten.

A herniated disk? Minor. Treatment is easy. What's that you say? The crappy workers compensation doctors could not figure out a fix? Suffer!

Over the years, the condition worsens. It is one disk. Now two. Now three. Now, every other disk throughout your neck and upper thoracic spine are messed. Then, guess what? They're all bad.

Welcome to hell. But wait. It's not fully warmed up yet.

Now, let's throw some gasoline and lighter fluid on that smoldering fire.

Depression sets in. Work is no longer rewarding. Hell, work is no longer enjoyable or merely tolerable. Management is filled with brown nosers whose sole goal is to make people miserable. Decisions are made to force your resignation. Who wants an injured employee anyway?

No, this story takes a much larger free fall. Depending on the work week and regulations, the constant physical demands make you overlook your health issues. You put the company's welfare and the production needed for the daily product ahead of what you need. Work, work, work. Drive the sled, slave. Get the crops plowed. Re-enter the 1800s, where all men are definitely not created equal in the eyes of the law.

The pain begins to become more than one can handle. But, the product needs completion. What's a little extra pain? The 40-hour work weeks fade, replaced by a constant 50-hour minimum week. You see this all too often. When something comes up, rather than assign the "glamour" staff members, more work is piled on the laborers like you. The bosses crack the whip, and you say "yes sir" and "no sir." That is the new way of business in America.

When the pain finally becomes too much and interferes with the job, you are maligned for loafing or causing problems. Your character undergoes an assassination. Everyone hears about how horrible you are and how much of a detriment you are to the company's overall bottom line.

Eventually, the company figures out a creative solution to end your employment, if one is needed. The simplest solution is to just fire someone outright. In situations where a reason must be provided, the creativity bubbles to the surface. Some will fire you for cause, citing your lack of ability to perform as a team player. Others will invent odd, yet convenient methods to achieve their goals. The company is downsizing, and the injured employee's position is somehow the one targeted for a reduction. This method is wonderful, as seniority or issues of importance can be tossed aside.

This is precisely what happened to me.

I fought through intense pain for years. And, after years and years of fighting, I planned on giving up.

THE ACCIDENT

How does one's life get sidetracked so quickly? It is easy. Some idiot doesn't know how to drive, and he mistakes a guy waving a flag as an officer of the law and cuts across an intersection.

Yep. It was that easy.

I was a passenger in a co-worker's car. We were on our way to cover the first game of Vince McMahon's football league, the XFL.

We were driving toward the stadium in Orlando to see some God awful football. Traffic was flowing. A parking attendant was waving his little flag toward the lot he was guarding. A 16-year-old sees the waving flag and decides to hit the gas. Surely, that was an invitation to him to cut across all the traffic lanes.

BAM! WHAM! CRASH! (Thanks for the inspiration, Adam West.)

I was looking down at the parking directions for the credential and never saw it coming. The moron struck the front passenger side of the car with the front driver's side of his SUV. I was the only one of seven people (three in our car and four in the SUV/tank) that wore a seatbelt. And, guess what? I was the only one who got injured. Yep. I followed Florida law and got screwed. Thanks Florida!

I instantly felt pain in my neck and right arm. My knee was hurt. I called the paper and told them about what happened.

Should I go to the hospital? No. Let me cover this abortion of a game so I can get a good headline and byline. It's all about the company and working my way up.

Of course I opted for the game. The company should come first. I'll be rewarded down the line, right? Yeah, good luck with that.

I returned home and sought out medical care from my doctor. I was then sent to the workers constipation (sorry compensation) office for an evaluation. The marvelous doctor there proceeded to jam my head against my shoulder despite me telling him it hurt to move it more than two inches. He went to push it the other way, and I slapped his hands away.

"Touch my [expletive] neck one more time, and I'll rip your arms off and beat you over the head with them."

Funny, I still remember my exact words at that moment. Maybe that was the seminal moment in my life, the moment when my body was telling me that my life was effectively over. I can almost picture my body telling my mind, 'You're done, buddy.'

MY BACKGROUND

I grew up in Hollywood, Florida, the son of Robert and Martha Emanuel. My younger brother Chris is mentally disabled, a source of most of what was good in my family.

My father worked as an airline mechanic for Eastern Airlines. The perks were great. I remember traveling to so many cool places as a child. Disney became engrained in me. The love of amusement parks grew with each passing year.

That joy was ultimately snatched from me in 1989. My father suffered an accident at work, one that would lead him to life on disability payments.

The trips were gone. Sure, we still went to Disney World in Orlando, but the California jaunts were over. The visits to parks in odd places came to a close. Happiness given only to be taken away. I should have realized right then and there as a child that lesson would become the guiding direction to my life.

A few years after my father's accident, I graduated from McArthur High School. I only sent one college application out, and it was to my beloved University of

Miami. Holy smoke! I got accepted. And I went to the school of the Hurricanes gladly. Life was good there. I had good friends, great teachers and a wonderful education. But that, too, changed. I realized in the middle of an all essay biology test in my sophomore year that pre-medicine was not right for me. My hopes and dreams of becoming a doctor were gone. Pulled away once again, like Lucy pulling the ball away from poor Charlie Brown time and again.

Needless to say, I dusted myself off.

I changed majors. I decided to become a journalist.

With the change in majors came a change in school. I opted to attend Florida International University in Miami. It was there that I met my friend Ryan. That's a good memory. I also met the guy who gave me my first journalism job, George Richards, there as well.

I started writing for the Miami Herald in the fall of 1996. I freelanced stories about high school football in Broward County. I made a good impression, as by January I was offered a staff position in the high school section.

I worked my way up, and I was asked to write a story about an odd contract the Miami Dolphins agreed to with cornerback Sam Madison in the spring of 2000. I did a great job. I asked questions the NFL had to answer. And I got noticed. My bosses realized I knew what I was doing. By the start of that football season, I was issued season credentials and began to cover my beloved Dolphins.

I experienced the great things life offered. I was with the big shots in the journalism field. I was with the elite. Most importantly, I was happy and my star was on the rise.

Who knew the fall would be plotted just six months later when the accident occurred?

Yep, happiness replaced by sadness. Quite the trend.

MY CAREER

How did I get to this point? Why didn't I see the warning signs? Why did I fight through pain when evidence suggested I should stop?

Much of my situation resulted from shoddy medical advice, which will be covered elsewhere in this manifesto. But, much of it was also from stubborn pride and the desire to do well in the field I chose.

The career was too alluring. It was too perfect. It was the ultimate gig for a sports junkie. I covered sports for the Miami Herald. And I was happy. And content.

I got to go to all the home games for the Miami Dolphins, my favorite team in all of sports. I got to cover the gridiron heroes I always admired. I got to go into the locker room and interact with the guys. I got to live the fan's ultimate dream. I was damn good at it too.

I also got to cover high school sports, which became a passion for me. These kids and coaches were pure. Coaches did this because they loved the sports, loved teaching kids and impacting lives. The athletes did this because they enjoyed it. Sure, some had professional aspirations and even more used sports as a vehicle to get a college education.

But the majority played because they loved it. Money was not an issue. Politics were not a topic either. Pure, unadulterated love – capped by the ultimate joy of success – was what most high school athletes were in search of.

This, of course, was the allure of covering the sports. I got to experience that joy from afar.

My career also afforded me the opportunity to get involved with a personal passion, mixed martial arts competitions.

While physically I was never more than a spectator, I loved the beauty and purity of the sport.

There was typically such an appreciation by the fighters. They were grateful for coverage. They were professionals. They supported each other. Even two fighters pitted against each other, who had just brutally beat one another for 15 minutes, embrace and congratulate each other on their accomplishments. Sportsmanship reigned supreme.

While at the Miami Herald, I typically worked 50-60 hour work weeks. It was long. It was arduous. At first, it was my pleasure. After time, however, it became my burden, my scarlet 'A' to display for the world to see.

The injuries changed everything. I went from eager to pick up additional assignments to trying to avoid the phone on my off time. The paper didn't care if I was hurt. They wanted their assignments covered. I get that from a pure labor standpoint. But have some compassion people.

My first screwed up thing came when I got a doofy boss from the Carolinas. He didn't want to work. He wanted to take the easy road. He found out I knew how to paginate, and he wanted me in the office. I had medical orders for field work of course, but Doofy didn't care. It led to some major fights, and it triggered the management to put me in their crosshairs.

I won that battle somehow and kept going. Why didn't I listen then and say enough is enough? I should have called it quits. I should have demanded more out of the medical personnel. No, instead I worked through things.

I eventually developed a target on me. I wasn't friendly with my co-workers. I wasn't a team player any longer. But, I wasn't a fool either. I knew I would be a target when we got information about 'Voluntary' withdrawals. I knew what this meant. Oh God. Help me.

I was notified that seniority meant nothing. My position was being eliminated. When another employee found out I was on the chopping block, he offered to take the buyout instead to save my job. Only problem is the guy - yes, I'm talking about you Mike Phillips - wanted me to pay him $10,000 or more. I declined the offer. I was let go.

After my time at the Miami Herald came to a close, and after legal wrangling which will be discussed later, I began a four-year campaign as a nationally syndicated columnist for Scripps Howard News Service.

While with Scripps, I was able to continue my coverage of mixed martial arts. I attended numerous events and forged strong contacts within the companies. Unfortunately, the company was bought out by McClatchy, and I was once again let go. That's two layoffs from the same company. It is almost inconceivable. Yet, it happened. People laugh when I tell them this, but it's so true.

Thanks McClatchy!

What are the chances of a double whammy like that? Yeah, my life is special.

WHO WILL HELP?

Before you begin to think there may be some salvation through medical and legal means, forget it.

The system is corrupt.

Doctors derive their income from the insurance companies. The patient complains of X, Y and Z. The doctor initially shows concern and tries to help. But, when the bills begin to pile up and real costs are associated with the pending treatment, the insurance company steps in and flexes its muscle.

Who knows how the system truly works?

Are the doctors told to play ball or else they lose their status as a provider for that company? Are the doctors given payouts to claim their loyalty and give an insurance-friendly report? Do the doctors give a damn about anything beyond their fat and ever expanding pockets?

The answer to those questions is a mystery, although the last question is answered with a resounding no. The doctors ultimately care about the doctors and their pockets.

One doctor told me I was diabetic. The cause for his astute medical discovery? I walked in and was fat. Stop the presses. I can write my own headline here. 'Miracle doctor in Hollywood diagnoses health issues without doing an exam.' Wow. Really?

Yet another doctor spent a total of 38 seconds with me. I was told 98 percent of those with injuries similar to mine did not have the level of pain I CLAIMED to. Yes, he used the word "claimed." Thank you for calling me a liar. It's not bad enough I am in more pain than I can handle. I really needed the emotional kick to the groin that comment provided.

Unfortunately, Mr. 38 Seconds wrote that I did not need many work restrictions. And the malicious liar that nearly ruined my life admitted he took the restrictions and "rubber stamped" it like so many of the doctors do. So, despite hearing my impassioned calls for help over insurmountable pain, this idiot admits to rubber stamping the recommendation of another doctor over the consistent cries for help from his own patient.

Can you sense a trend? I had yet another doctor put me off work. He had restrictions on me for months until he deemed my condition too painful and severe to work. So, he sat me during football season - my favorite time of the work year. Yeah, it was the busiest, but I enjoyed those few months more than any other. Anyway, back to Dr. Head-in-his-Rectum. He sent me for epidural injections in my neck. During the time I was out, my MRI exam confirmed my condition worsened. The doctor felt the epidurals would work wonders since he himself underwent that treatment and was fine afterward. When I went, nothing happened. No improvement. No change. A null gain. So, what does the top notch surgeon do? Puts me back to work, removes the restrictions and refuses to talk to me. Yeah, he received a death threat from me. Wouldn't you do the same? I thought so!

When situations like this happen, what choices do you, the patient and chronic sufferer, have? Well, you can fight it, of course. But, in my case, I was weary. I had fought the fight for nearly a decade. Considering I was only 35 at the time, more than a quarter of my life had been spent in pain – including more than half of my adult life. And those ratios will only go up.

I fought the good fight. I battled. I did all I could. When was it enough? At what point do you wave the white flag? That is the final battle, the one I'm engaged in right now. The flag is ready to fly. It's just a matter of waving it at this point.

There were a few Hail Mary options left, however, that could keep that proverbial flag at bay.

Of course, my lawyer could work some sort of magic. He was a good guy, the type that really wanted to see his clients put in the best situation. (I later found out he helped embezzle $60 million in a Ponzi scheme. Yikes!)

With so many people in the legal or medical field, you get the sense that it is all about them and what they can get from you. With this guy, I got the sense he was in the battle with me, pushing to make my pathetic life better. He was fighting for me. That was so true. I felt like I had given up the fight. Yet, there he was, fighting for me.

What tricks can he pull out? What options are left? When you have the scum of the earth, better known as medical professionals on the pay roll of the evil insurance companies, there are not many plays one can make.

Fortunately, there was a sliver of hope. The psychiatrist on the case, one who has seemed to fully support me over the insurance dictators, could sway this battle and ultimately lead me to win the war.

He was a bright and pure beacon. He never seemed to say the company line and endorse the insurance companies. He asked questions and shared his personal history. He tried to make sessions more like friendly conversations.

Now, here is where he will undergo his ultimate test.

Does he support me? Does he feel like I am telling the truth about the pain and the associated mental problems that have arisen because of the pain? These answers will determine how much longer I would be here. If he helps, as I thought he would, then I had hope. If he stood on the sideline and merely pushed the situation along, I'm done. My life will be over. It is a lot of power for one man to wield, yet it is there for him to wield nonetheless.

Guess what? He did not disappoint me. He actually gave a damn about me. What? Really? But he was being paid by comp. But there he was, pushing for me to get what I needed.

I always felt indebted to him after that.

THE DECISION

I remember the first day I decided I was going to take my own life.

Oh, it was to be simple.

My doctor, assigned by workers compensation, ordered a morphine pump to be placed under the skin in my stomach. The hockey puck sized piece of metal was to provide a steady drip of morphine directly to my spine. This was to numb whatever pain was there and allow me to live a more normal life.

The doctor cautioned I would never be well enough to resume a work schedule with the pump. Basically, it looked like either I spend the rest of my life disabled or spend it disabled and in less pain.

Despite the allure, I opted not to have the pump. I'm not fond of drugs, nor do I enjoy the feelings associated with them. I told the doctor no. He said he understood, and we would look for another option.

A few days later, I discovered the deceitful doctor lied to my face and gave a report to comp that I was fine. My lawyer called me to his office. My dad and I went. It was then my lawyer told me how screwed I was.

Did I get upset? No. Instead I was unexplainably calm and collected. It was like a wave of peace washed over me. I knew what needed to be done, and I was fine with my decision.

My lawyer was concerned. Why was I so calm? Simple. I revealed my plan. I was taking my gun to the doctor's parking lot. I have two clips. One was being emptied directly into his skull. I'd change clips, and I would then put a single shot into my own. Told you it was simple. It was not revenge. It was justice.

My lawyer talked me out of it. Well, at least he thought he did.

I sat on my couch that night with the loaded gun on my lap. I was ready. It was time. Then a friend kept calling. She wouldn't take no for an answer. She knew something was wrong, and she was determined to come over and make sure I didn't do anything stupid.

I told her to come over and see the body.

She rushed over there as fast as she could. The door was unlocked. She came in, and I hid the gun under the couch's cushion. I told her to leave, but she would have none of it. She dragged me into the shower, got me dressed and took me out.

I didn't do it that night. But I have thought of it nearly every day since.

GOVERNMENT REACTION

Why has it all reached this point, you may ask?

Simple. Everything about the country we live in is corrupt. The political system is a sham. Nothing is designed to work right. Why do we get fired up over which candidate wins and what their views are? No matter if we elect the reanimated corpses of George Washington and Abraham Lincoln or if we put another southern buffoon like George Bush in the White House, nothing will change.

The system, originally designed to govern us, has been manipulated and twisted. Nothing gets done. Politicians discovered ways to slow the system to a crawl, better maximizing their potential to get donations and pay offs. Why would anyone want to bust their tail to get into a job where the benefits, officially that is, are so poor? Easy. No one would do it. Instead, these scumbags figured out how to line their pockets with money. Would a law be beneficial to the people? Who cares? Who will line the pockets of the politicians? Suddenly, they care.

The government set up a system for the injured where nothing works.

In worker's compensation, for example, the only medical opinions that matter are those of the doctors paid for by the worker's compensation carriers.

Think about that for a minute. The insurance company selects the doctor and pays the doctor. The doctor writes his report. The patient goes through the sham process. Ultimately, the report surfaces to support the insurance company. The patient's best interests are forgotten. You're manipulated once again.

Want to bring your own doctor's opinions to the plate? Get the view of someone not in the employ of the evil empire? Sorry, it can't happen.

The only medical opinion that carries weight in these cases is that one of the doctor employed by the insurance company. Talk about being judge, jury and – as is often and unfortunately the case – executioner.

A HAIL MARY ANSWERED

Just when all seemed darkest, and the end was closing in, I got some good news.

My lawyer got the insurance company to switch doctors, and I was okay for a bit longer. A settlement was worked out. Another lawyer pushed for a Social Security Disability hearing, which I got after a few months.

Even then, I thought I was done just 30 seconds into the hearing. The judge told my lawyer to stop reading his opening statement. This cannot be good.

The judge asked me several generic questions. Then he told me it was hard to award me Disability when I put in for it the month after I was laid off. But wait. If I amended my onset date to the following year, things looked good.

My lawyer and I stepped out. He told me what just happened. I already knew. Thirty seconds later, we were back in the chambers agreeing to the new deal.

I took my settlement and moved on. I began to write a nationally syndicated column on mixed martial arts for

Scripps Howard News Service, and I was happy. It gave me a connection to my past life.

I followed my parents up to Clermont, Florida. I loved the area. I enjoyed the people. At least I did at first. It was lonely. It was boring. But it was new, and I was away from all the craziness.

Was I finally past this depression stage? I believed so. I stopped taking medication for a while, and I generally felt fine.

But, once this damn disease takes hold of you, the thing never lets go.

GOD AND RELIGION

Pray on it, you are told.

Help will be offered.

Divine intervention is the key. He will not abandon you.

As the comic duo Penn and Teller said in their hit Showtime series, this is all BS!

If there truly was some divine figure, some authority who can help bend the whims and situations of the mortals under His domain, He surely has an odd way of inspiring faith.

Wars are rampant across our planet. Famine. Disease. Torture. Hunger. Suffering. All are present and major issues. What about natural disasters or supposed Acts of God? Yeah, that surely inspires faith that the God Almighty is looking down upon us with a helpful hand. Perhaps he is, and humanity is just his favorite toy to mess with. Can't you just hear the thought process now? "Let's see, Haiti is a place where people live like hell and suffer daily. Ummm, earthquake. Yeah. That would be a hoot. Let's see what happens!" Somehow, I don't think the grand architect of the universe would be so callous. He couldn't be. Or could he? Hmmm. Let's think about this for a minute.

If there is a God, why would He allow someone like me to be screwed over like this? Wouldn't He reward my dedication, my attempts to help fellow mankind and my attempts to do right by my family? Wouldn't He step in while I was getting screwed right and left? Wouldn't He make things right?

You would think the answer would be yes. But, I never got that answer personally. I still don't know if there is a deity. I will never know.

It baffles me that people put so much faith into an unknown entity. They worship weekly. They pray several times a day. They read their Bible or appropriate facsimile of it depending on their respective religion. They throw money into the donation jar.

Ah. There it is.

Religion is about the donations, pure and simple. It's about paying for the pastor's new car. The Catholic church has amassed more wealth in the Vatican than most countries possess. There is gold everywhere. They say they're about helping those in need, but every time they speak they have their hands out. Sure, they'll help those in need with my money, but will they dip into their fur-lined coffers and take anything out? Hell no. But, yet, they tell us to respect God and to worship him.

I've prayed to God numerous times.

I've never seen my prayers answered.

Religion? To quote the great Scrooge McDuck, "Bah humbug."

I don't believe in this concept, and - short of a miracle - I never can. The Force in Star Wars sounds more plausible than religion. But, at least in Star Wars, I know it's part of a story designed for entertainment, and the fine folks at Disney are more than happy to reach into my pocket with the Force to pry away my money.

THE BREAKING POINT

Perhaps the worst component of the contemplation of suicide comes in the most unexpected area – from the ones who are closest to you.

Friends scoff at your pain levels. Other people have it worse they say. It is impossible to convey how poorly you feel to others. Imagine being in so much pain that you literally must go to the bathroom to vomit. Imagine this happening at least once every 10 days. Your pain is just that intense.

You have all seen videos of torture, whether it is Hollywood inspired or real life stuff. The toughest people on the planet eventually crack under the massive weight of pain and suffering. These people reach a point where they can simply not tolerate any additional pain. Do whatever you have to do. Just make it stop. They have reached their individual breaking points. No more pain or torture can be tolerated. Make it end now. Do whatever you can to call for the end, no matter what the cost or consequence.

Yet, despite reaching this breaking point, outsiders think you can just push through it. When they suggest nonsense such as that, you try to explain. But, resistance is returned. It can't be as bad as you say. No, you can get through it. Just ignore the pain. Nonsense. Try ignoring the pain of a 500-pound weight resting on your foot. Just sit there. Eventually the pain will fade away. Guess what. It doesn't. It hurts more as it crushes your bones, decimates your soft tissue and causes irreparable damage. Yet, the uninformed and healthy ones can give this advice over and over. Let them experience your level of pain for just 10 minutes. Watch how quickly they would buckle and beg to end the experiment.

Perhaps this is why the Saw movies are so popular. People in the movies must push through immense pain to survive. But guess what. If they do make it past the pain, it ends. Cut off an arm to live. Sucks, but once it is done and the bleeding is stopped, that character is just a one-armed bandit.

Translate that to real life though. You pushed through the pain. You took the first slice off, just the tip of the finger. Now, you have to continually slice. Yes, your hand and arm are on one of those butcher machines, where they maneuver the meat back and forth making cut after cut after cut. How many people could survive that process and say to keep cutting? Not many. Is it even possible?

Yet, that is what you're told as a chronic pain sufferer. Just keep taking off slices. You can get by with a quarter inch less of your arm. Oh, it hurts? Well, it's only another quarter inch today. And, guess what. Tomorrow is yet another quarter inch on the slicer.

At some point, you say enough. End the slicing. End the torture. End whatever must be ended to make the pain stop. If it means the end of life, so be it. Just make the suffering stop.

This is often the watershed moment, the time when one must decide if living truly is worth the price one must pay.

I would venture when others reach this breaking point, the decision more often than not results in some sort of fatality. This is a difficult point to reach, a point that requires great pain over a long period of time. When one reaches this point, the decision to end the fight is viewed more as the sane choice rather than the insane one.

PROBLEMS RESURFACE

Things were great in Clermont - at first. I was happy with the family. I was happy with the area.

But then, it started to change. I had left all my friends to come here. I left my life.

Loneliness crept in. It enveloped me eventually. I couldn't escape my own head. The depression came back. Slowly, like a damp mist, it ensnared me in its clutches and surrounded me.

I met a wonderful woman, who lived in South Florida. She created a sense of euphoria in my life. When I was with her, things were wonderful and my life seemed complete. When I was apart from her, however, the depression was worse than ever before. The lows without her were horrendous. I couldn't take those lows for long.

I asked her about moving up with me. I offered to let her, her son and her mother live with me, rent free. All I asked was that she give up her highly-paid job as a dancer and move up to be with me. She could get a regular 9-to-5 job somewhere and bring in $2-3,000 per month. My disability benefits would cover the house's expenses (phone, TV, internet, electric, taxes, insurance, etc.). Her money would allow us to live a very comfortable life, one that would pay for our purchases, food, care for her son and other assorted odds and ends. It would allow us to create a savings account together and save up for her son's college fund.

Alas, she said things were too soon. She didn't want to leave the money. I was devastated.

But then she explained the reasons why she had to continue to make money. This poor woman was going through an emotional hell. I felt horrible that I even questioned her motivations. She had to do this. It was necessary.

The fact that she had a great guy willing to provide for her in every way, shape and form - a guy willing to overlook her issues and accept her for what she was - did not sway her. It couldn't.

Ultimately, while she says frequently that she loves me, I don't know if she in sincere. That uncertainty is killing me, quite possibly literally.

I'm feeling suicidal thoughts again, and the allure is strong. I'm trying to be strong. I would hate to devastate my parents and brother. I would hate to disappoint my friends and loved ones. And, finally, I would hate to possibly hurt the special woman in my life. If she was sincere and meant what she told me, this act would destroy her in every sense, especially when she finds out how much my stability hinged on her relationship with me. It simply hurts me to my very core knowing I could cause her such pain.

Unfortunately, as strong as I try to be, the possibility of ending it all is simply too strong.

The pain can finally end. The suffering can be over. I wouldn't have to hurt any longer. I wouldn't have to feel the pangs in my heart. I would finally feel peace and tranquility. If there is an afterlife, I would hope I'd be viewed for all my positive contributions, including my past year as a Mason, rather than the perceived cowardly way I would end things. This was not the way I wanted it to go, but circumstances were what they were.

A sudden gall bladder surgery recently only further messed up my emotions. I realized how mortal I was. I realized I was going to be 40 in just eight months, and I had nothing to show for it other than material crap. I didn't have a wife. I didn't have any kids. I just had myself, and that is nothing special.

To further exacerbate my problems, there were further complications from the stomach issue. It's been nearly two months since I first felt the onset of a problem, and I've dropped 35 pounds in that time span. There's something majorly wrong.

My appetite is gone. I enjoyed food in the past. You don't cross the 300-pound barrier and not be a fan of food. Now, I cannot eat. And when I do, I have to run to the bathroom once or twice in the next 10-20 minutes. It's almost like there is a small tank in my stomach. Add new stuff to the tank to top it off and then let the runoff flow on out. Hey, it's better than it was before. Then, I'd eat and have diarrhea the rest of the day. As of today, it's a decent sized lunch followed by a nearly non-existent dinner. Isn't life grand? One of the few pleasures I had left in life is now gone. Yeah, there are so many reasons for me to stick around this rock.

FEELING TRAPPED

Whenever I spoke to anyone (see details in the next chapter), I was forced to explain why I felt the way I felt. What could be so bad to get me to do this? Isn't there something that could be done?

As answered elsewhere in this manifesto, the answer is a resounding no.

I am trapped in my financial situation. I make a certain amount through Disability. It is enough money to survive, even with my parents' help. But it is not enough money to live. There is a huge difference.

I did everything right. I was on track to pay off my house by age 35. I would have had a three-year-old car. But, no. I got laid off. I went on Disability. My nest egg never got built. I could have survived this at age 45. Not at age 35.

As the final days approached, it felt like I was in a cage. The walls were closing in. No matter what I do, I cannot escape the financial reality. It sucks. If I get Baker Acted, it will help for a few days. When I get out, I'll still be in the same position.

I had some opportunities in my final months. I was
asked to write for a magazine. Unfortunately, the owner
couldn't find his way out of a paper bag, and that fizzled.
I thought of starting my own publication, but was
properly discouraged by a friend. I was invited to join a
charitable organization which could pay me a decent
salary to be its writer/public relations officer. That has
yet to come to fruition.

I am tired of fighting the finances. My father offered to
help, but I cannot take any more of his money.

On top of that, I want to take care of the love of my life.
I want to help her through what she is going through. It
is the only thing that matters to me in these final days.
I'm thinking of cashing my bank accounts out and
bringing her the money soon. Let my final act benefit
someone. I'll take her on a trip for two weeks. The cash
will cover her missed work and then some.

I will give her a story that I won some money in the
Powerball drawing. I want to give her some. I want to
take her away to celebrate a bit. Get a great trip in. Her
and I could spend what amounts to my final days on
earth on the road together. The euphoria from the time
away with her will be tremendous. When it is over, the
time away from her will be overbearing. It will be too
much for me to take. It will help me over the hump.

This may be the best idea I ever had. She gets a good amount of money to help her. I'll experience one final boost of joy, which will translate to one final depressive ditch. Sounds perfect. It's a win-win. I get time with my love, and I get to experience living - truly living - one last and final time. She gets a few weeks with me that she will remember the rest of her life and an outstanding vacation. She gets a good amount of cash (more than $10,000). When we part, I know it will be the last time I ever see her, and I did my part to make her life better. It will also be the final day of my life. I cannot think of any better way to go out.

My sacrifice will mean something. At least I can take some solace in that.

LIVING VS. SURVIVING

One of the topics and phrases I've used with friends is Living vs. Surviving. I figured it needed its own section to explain what I mean.

I had a great life at one point. I covered Miami Dolphin games routinely. I was at some Miami Heat games. I was always at different high school events. Things were great. I was out a lot, and I was at different sporting events that - while technically work - were actually pretty fun.

I traveled frequently. I was in California or Las Vegas every summer (sometimes both). I enjoyed living the life I had.

Once I went on Disability, I realized my situation allowed me merely to survive. Gone was the extra travel income. Gone was the constant sporting events. Without money to afford tickets, gone was even the occasional sporting events.

I couldn't spend money on things I wanted to. I had to be frugal. I had to be responsible. This was fine for a few years. I realized this is what I had to do to make it through the months. Eventually though, I realized this was a death sentence of sorts. I was alive, yes. But I was no longer living. To me, this is a big difference. And, to me, that is the ultimate difference between life and death.

I'm built to live. I cannot merely survive.

WHAT IT FEELS LIKE

Friends and loved ones show concern when I discuss this issue with them. But they typically ask that one question that is so hard to answer - What does it feel like?

I have not been able to verbalize this to anyone yet, and I think it may be easier to write about it.

Imagine feeling happiness for a few minutes, just out of randomness. All of a sudden, the happiness is replaced by despair. You watch TV or a movie, or you listen to music, and something just pulls on your heartstrings. I had not cried in years. I cried probably two dozen times in the last three months. I never got emotional at movies. Now, I feel myself swell up.

When the despair hits, it chokes you. You feel your heart racing. Your mind gets foggy. You feel run down. Things seem out of place. You cannot find any happiness, no matter what you do. I am a huge fan of the NFL Draft. I have watched every pick since 1988. To me, it's more exciting than the Super Bowl - probably because my beloved Dolphins never appear there. I watched the Draft the last few nights, and I gleaned zero entertainment or joy from it. You must understand, I

53

wait all year for this thing. I obsess over it. I make charts, do research, make spreadsheets, etc. This is my personal, three-day holiday. So far, through two days, I could care less. That disturbs me, and more importantly, that worries me.

The despair has other physical effects on you. I feel myself slouched over. I feel the drag on my face. I feel the slow hitch in my step. Something just feels amiss.

You try to shake the feeling, but it is inescapable. It surrounds you. It envelops you.

For reasons such as this, I turned to substances to try to help. I have smoked some marijuana. I drank. I took pills. I experimented with a combination of the three. Does it work? Oh yeah. But it only works for a little while. Eventually, the high or buzz wears off. And the 'eventually' is much quicker with major, deep depression. Some relief, however, is better than none.

It also helps to talk to friends. It gets your mind off things. It lets you put yourself in their world. Their pleasure becomes your pleasure for the slightest moment. It is nearly a symbiotic relationship for a brief period.

Alas, even those temporary fixes do not matter much. It seems, to me at least, that when the good feelings from the above items wears off, you return to that major depressive state much harder. You know you're doing damage to your body. You just don't care. You need relief. You crave it. It doesn't matter how stupid you know your actions are. You need that relief and are determined to do damn near anything to get it.

Throughout the episode, drowsiness sets in. You feel yourself growing tired by the moment. It is almost like a noose has been draped across your neck, and the tug becomes more and more real. You can almost feel yourself blacking out.

When things get really bad, you think about your death. It hurts me greatly to think of my mother crying at my casket, hunched over, wailing 'Why' and saying she can't believe I'd do this to her. I can think of my love getting the news and slumping to the ground, tears streaking down her beautiful face, absolute horror crippling her. I can think of my handicapped brother who will not understand what happened and why his beloved brother is no longer here. It will be most difficult for him, and that realization makes me feel lower than dog crap. He will never understand. While others can read this manifesto and see things through my eyes, my brother will never have that luxury. All he will know is his brother, his friend and his companion is gone, never to be seen by him again. I can think of my poor father, who I burdened by telling him all of this, sitting there, crying, wondering what more he could have done to help. Dad, rest assured, you did everything you could. There was nothing more you could do. You were great to me my whole life. I know we fought and butted heads all the time, but I hope you know how much I loved you. You were my rock, and I am forever grateful for how you raised me and what you provided me with.

The thought of your own death is frightening. No one wants to die before their time. No one wants to cut their life short. It's at times like this though that I remember depression truly is a disease. It is a crippling, unmerciful beast unlike anything else. While cancer eats away at your physical body, depression eats away at your soul. Even though others cannot see my deterioration, I can feel it. Each passing day I sink further and further. It is almost like I'm standing in a pool of quicksand, and each second that passes brings me closer and closer to the bottom. It's just a matter of time before it overtakes my head and chokes me out, bringing about my death.

How will I be remembered? That's a tough one. But it's something I think about. I would hope people will look at me and remember my good qualities. They can remember the type of friend I was to them. They can remember how I made them laugh. They can remember how I was there to support them when they were going through bad times. They can remember how I made other people feel like they were stars around me. At least, that's how I hope they remember me. I'm not sure how the final score on my soul will be tallied. I hope I grade out positively, for that is how I strived to live my life.

If I could pick the words that best describe me, from my perspective at least, I would say:

Funny.
Intelligent.
Compassionate.
Friendly.
Supportive.
Complicated.
Dark.
Depressed.

That's a good list at first. Then it gets scary. And that is what this depression feels like. From good to bad in five seconds flat. Happy. Sad. Euphoric. Devastated. Alive. Dead?

I sit here and wish there was a way out. I have prayed to God that I win Powerball. I have begged, pleaded, bargained and promised. I know it won't help. I already said I don't really believe in religion. But everyone keeps telling me to look to the Bible for answers. I am, in my own unique way. If there truly is a God, and he is as powerful as his believers say, why can't he help me? I did right. I did good. I never screwed anyone over. I never hurt anyone. I was innocent and got hurt because of someone else's negligence. Why do I have to suffer?

And that's part of this crap too. Why do I have to suffer? You ask yourself that question constantly. Why me? What did I do to deserve this? It sucks. It almost becomes your mantra. Why me?

And that is precisely how this damn thing feels.

FIGHTING OFF MR. D

A good friend of mine, who is suffering from terminal cancer and will not likely live through the year, gave me some advice recently. Ben calls depression 'Mr. D', and he told me how he deals with it.

"I tell that mother [expletive] to leave me alone," Ben said.

It sounds good. It sounds like logical advice. Unfortunately Ben, we're wired differently.

I have tried to tell this damn disease to go screw itself. I truly have. It just has a hold on me and is clutching with every last possible ounce of fight.

I sought medical advice. I talk about my problems. I'm open. I'm honest. Yet, the damn Mr. D just won't release its grip on me.

Ben is a strong, proud man. He has fought this for nine years. He's won. He looked cancer in the face and flipped it off. Originally told he would make it a few years, Ben outlived the estimate and is nearing year 10 with this thing. He's fought off depression the whole time. Imagine being told you were going to be eaten alive from the inside and that you had a few years to live. Depression would have gotten a hold of me then and never let go. I don't know how he managed to live this long and how he managed to fight this off. I wish I had that strength.

I told Mr. D where to go, but he just will not leave. Sorry I could not be as strong as you Ben.

A SIGN

I did not plan this entry, but something on television just caught my attention and forced a 3 a.m. addition.

During the penultimate episode of the current season of Person of Interest on CBS, a person is arrested and falsely accused of a crime. While he is incarcerated, the person decides to take his own life.

His brother is asking for an explanation. He demands one.

The government lackey tells him, "Innocent people don't kill themselves Mr. Brandt."

His brother responds, "No, people without hope do. And you robbed him of that."

I don't know who wrote this episode, but that one, singular exchange was more profound that most people realize. It spoke straight to my heart. I watched the scene a few times. I felt the pain. I felt the sting. It hurt.

I am rarely moved by something on TV. This line, and the scene, really got me. It caused me to get up off the couch, head to the office and pull up the file to add this entry. Yes, it was powerful. It was telling. And, most of all, it was so damn accurate.

Think of that. People without hope take their own lives. How profound!

That's precisely what happens. In my case, I had hope of a great life. I was on the path toward one. A paid off house by age 35? Unheard of. Yet, it was there in my grasp. I did the right thing. I was full of hope.

Then, a little accident came along. Not too bad in the grand scheme of things. How bad could it really be?

Oh, how I wish I could have foregone the worker's compensation angle and had my own doctors treat me. I would be normal today. I would have a good life. I'd have a great job. I'd probably be married and would have a few Baby Bobs running around. Instead, I sit here in a dark office and write about how I want to kill myself.

My hope is gone. I'm destined to fail. There's no avoiding it. Sure, I can fight the urge. I fight it every damn day. I truly do. Things could be going fine, and my day seems good, but something on TV, in a movie or song or any other form of entertainment will bother me. Sometimes, there is no trigger. I'll just sit here, bored, by myself and think. Then, the sickness takes over. The pain sets in. The thought of suicide pokes its ugly head out of the shadows. It encompasses me, and it welcomes me. It feels like a friend, greeting me with open arms, welcoming me to enjoy a party with him.

People without hope kill themselves.

And, I lost my hope.

POTENTIAL FINAL DAYS

I have debated this for months. Years. Should I do it? Should I end it?

I fought the urge. I did. I reached out to friends and loved ones. I sought medical help. I did everything one can think of. Did it work? I don't know. I won't know. Unfortunately, this work will never be complete. How can I type the words 'I did it' from the grave? It's impossible.

As I contemplate my existence and decide what to do, I'll detail the actions I took in what could be my last days on earth. It could help the next person if it doesn't help me.

I wrote out my last will and testament.

I began to tell my closest friends. It scared them. It shocked them. It hurt them. But, they listened. They absorbed. They asked questions, and they offered advice and help. They were all-stars for me. I hope I ultimately do not let them down. Thank you Sam, JD, Kevin, Mike, Ryan, Jay, Chyna, Dani, Ben, Damien, Jaime, Jason, Dylan and George. You all rocked for me.

I called my psychiatrist and got in there. I got new medicine, and I started taking it. Oh, the shame of seeking help. It cripples me. But I did it. I had to. I'm a fighter, and I want to stay here. Thank you Barry.

I then told the love of my life. I'm not naming her for reasons that only two people know. I have to protect her. I swore an oath. Even from the grave, my protection must remain for her.

She was shocked when I told her. She was hurt. She cried. She asked me not to do it. But she allowed me to say what I had to say. She supported me. I think she understood. I promised her I would not do it. I promised her I would always be here for her. Unfortunately, this was the first and only lie I ever told her. But it was the biggest. I could not commit to stay here for anyone. I'm fighting it, yes, but I cannot make this one promise. It is unfair for me to even think I could. But I said it to reassure her. Surprisingly, for a few days at least, it reassured me. Funny how love works. Thank you, my love.

I was a member of the Masonic Lodge in Groveland, Florida, and I reached out to our Worshipful Master with my problems. He is a doctor, and he deals with situations like this frequently. He told me to visit him in his office for free. Come get his love and support. Come take a medicine that could help me. Finally get some relief. It sounded wonderful. It truly did. I'm glad I made the call. Will I get to try the medicine? I don't know. Depends how long I'll be around. Thank you Allan. And thank you to my fellow Brothers for welcoming me and making me part of your family.

I called my old psychologist, now a dear family friend. I told him what I was experiencing. He pledged his support. He expressed his love. He offered encouragement. I knew he would. He was a great man who overcame many difficulties in his life. Thank you Randy.

I told my father to remove the gun from my house and promised him an explanation. I did not want to tell my mother. She would not understand. She could not understand. She would cry. She would beg me to get help. She would make me feel even worse. But, my father is different. He is smart. He is loving. He doesn't show that side at times, but he cares about me. I know that. It was hard to tell him what I'm dealing with. But I did. I think he understood my position. Obviously, he doesn't want me to do it. But he understands. Hopefully, in time, he can make my mother understand. Thank you, dad.

My most telling moment came on the day I may have saw my love for the last time. I was lucky enough to go to dinner with her last night. We had some drinks. I got tipsy. I asked to stay over at her hotel, and she said yes. I know she didn't want me there that night. But she accommodated me anyway. She is just that kind of woman. Again, thank you my love.

But this morning, during a conversation with JD, something just overwhelmed me. I believe I found inner peace for the first time in a long time. Subconsciously, over the past few months, I made amends with people that have angered me. I didn't know why. I just did it. Then it hit me.

People call those who commit suicide a coward. They say it's the easy way out. Let me tell you something. It's downright courageous. Do you have any idea how hard it is to sit there with a loaded gun on your lap, thinking you could end it all. The pain you will cause others is immense. It is incomprehensible. But if you can do it, you overcame the last hurdle of your test.

Right after saying that, I had the epiphany.

I compared myself to a cancer patient. Some did not get the comparison. I found it scary, accurate and disturbing. But I found it true and real. So real.

If you have a loved one suffering from cancer - or any other fatal disease - you know what I'm talking about. Seeing them wither away, suffering, dying in front of you is heart wrenching. You feel their pain with them. You cannot escape it.

With those diseases, you can see your loved ones withering away. With depression, which is a real S.O.B. of a disease, it is hard to see the onset and deterioration. But it is real. It exists.

As with cancer, when your loved one finally passes, you gain a sense of relief. They are no longer suffering. Their misery is over. Death becomes a release. Instead of tragedy, it is met with a strange mix of emotion. But the main emotion is peace. You're glad they are not spending another minute in the hell they were in. Depression is the same way. Or, at least, it should be viewed that way. If I do this, please do not view this as a sad and tragic occurrence. View it the way it should be viewed. My pain is over. My struggle is over. I found peace. Celebrate that essential truth. I'm sure there will be tears. I'm sure there will be a feeling of devastation to many. I'm sure it will be hard. But, please, remember this is my salvation. This is my peace. My pain ends. I can finally rest.

If I do decide to end things once and for all, let this entire manifesto serve as my suicide note. It was intended to be such from the beginning, going back to 2009 when the depression first reached its crescendo. While I did not open this file for many years, the feeling is back. My will to live has waned. Suicide, which was banished from my head for so long, is back with its allure of a quick end to the pain.

It's ringing my doorbell right at this very moment. And I'm thinking of opening the door and letting it in.

I'm sorry Mom. I'm sorry Dad. I'm sorry Chris. I'm sorry, my love. Ultimately, it is the four of you that have kept me here this long. It is the four of you that make this so hard to do. It is the four of you that I will hurt the most, but it is the four of you that will ultimately understand. I will miss the four of you the most. It's just my luck. I found true love finally, but it had to come in my final days.

Please, everyone, forgive me if I'm not strong enough to pull through this. I am trying. I truly am. But, if I cannot deal with this any longer and succumb to the pressure and pain, please know how difficult the decision was to end things and please find it in your hearts to eventually forgive me. I'm so sorry.

And to any of those who found solace or inspiration in my words, I wish you the best. Please be strong. Please do your best to win your struggles, whether that means you take your life or you show a different strength to continue to live. It is your individual choice. You will find the strength to make that choice when the time is right for you. If you do decide to leave the planet, find a way to impact someone you love and leave a legacy with them. Help them in ways you could not help them with while you were alive. Let your death mean something. To check out without that is a waste.

Good bye.

NOT SO FAST

So just when I think my decision is made, it gets difficult again.

I thought I was going to end it tonight. I really did. I still want to. I just drank a few shots of Jagermeister's new cinnamon and vanilla brew. It reminds me of my girlfriend. It reminds me of the good in life, the part of life that makes me smile, the part of life that makes me feel alive.

She is the thing keeping me here. It comes back to her, time and time again. I would be dead by now if it were not for her. I love her so much. I cannot do this to her. Not her. She is beautiful, and she is wonderful. She is the type of person that makes life worth living for, just to be around her. If I ever do go through with this, I hope she can read this and know how much she meant to me. If you do read this, please know that I love you. I do. I love you more than life itself. You are everything to me, and you are the only reason I have not swallowed a bottle of pills and downed 20 shots. If it were not for you, that would be done, and I'd be in a morgue.

Please know, my love, that it is because of you that I fight. It is because of you that I try. I was so ready to wave the white flag and surrender. It would be best for me and for those around me. It is the noble way to go. It is the best thing I can do. It may be the only thing I can do.

But, alas, because of you, I try. Because of you, I breathe today. Because of you, I deal with this monumental hurt and pain so grievous that few on this planet can understand. I began to pray, and I'm not religious. I have turned everything I know upside down, and I'm fighting. I truly am. I'm fighting every damn day, and I'm fighting every damn minute. My love, my struggle is for you. I hope you don't mind me putting this out there for all to see. But, it is my love for you that keeps me sucking in air.

I started a new project today. I made it to that project because of my love. The new project could be my salvation. It could deliver me from death's door and convince me to live. It could answer my hopes and dreams and allow me to provide for my love, to make her happy, to make her feel the way she should feel. I'm going to give this a little time. If it works, it would be wonderful and joyous. If it doesn't, despair will never be higher. If it doesn't, my decision is final. My death will await me. It is that simple. Either this project succeeds and I make money, or I end my life. There is no other option. It is one or the other. I've been disappointed so many times that I just feel the dread creeping in. It's there. It's always there. It never leaves. But, if this works, holy crap, I could be saved. Salvation may arrive. Maybe those prayers could help.

The new project centers around a charitable endeavor. But there is the production side of things that can be lucrative. A magazine, newsletter, video platform, website, etc. will all be part of it, and I'll get a piece of the action for my work. Now the guy running it seems like a good man. He seems honest. He seems legitimate. He seems like the kind of person who gives a crap about me, and he wants to help me in my situation. I think he understands the gravity of my situation. For, it is truly grave. Get it? Double meaning. Ah, moving on.

If this thing performs the way he thinks it should, I should be able to put a few grand in my pocket within the next 30-45 days. It will be glorious. Some of the money will go to my love. Some of it will go into my savings. But, my savings ultimately will belong to my love, so I'm doing this for her. The guy thinks we can ultimately make very, very good money doing this. I hope and pray he is right.

It looks like more chapters remain, and my fight will go on. How much longer it goes, I cannot be certain. But there will be more written.

If this story ends suddenly, and nothing more is said, you know the ultimate resolution of my problems. I will not be here. I will be in a coffin somewhere, at least what is left of me will be. I haven't decided how I will do it. The pills and alcohol thing seemed like a pretty good idea. Then of course there's always a 90 mile-per-hour crash into a tree or pole or wall or truck. That will do the trick as well. Yes, I've thought about it. I'm pissed I gave my father my gun. That would have been easy. Messy, but easy. I nearly did it once. Why not get to that point again?

The part that sucks is I feel like I'm being a nuisance to my friends. They probably look at their phones and consider sending me to voice mail. Hell, that's what I would do. The fact that they answer the phone, talk to me, encourage me, etc., shows me how much they truly care about me. They love me. They really do. And I appreciate that so, so much.

I did try to tell my mother about things today. She didn't really get my hints. I couldn't come out and just say, 'Hey mom, I may kill myself soon. If I do, I'm sorry.' How do you say that to your mother? It was hard telling my father. Don't get me wrong. But my father is much more stable. He is very aware of what's going on. He is cognizant of things. My mother? Errr, not so much. She is letting age creep in. Her faculties are not what they once were. She cannot accept this, nor will she understand. How could she? How could my father understand? Yet, somehow, he did. I'm shocked. I'm amazed. That was so cool of him to hear me out, and I will forever be grateful.

Maybe I should go out back and smoke a bowl of weed. That would help get me out of this mood, wouldn't it? I think it may.

I'm trying to be so positive today. I worked today. I wrote. I was a functioning member of society. For one day, I did what I needed to do. I was alive. Yes, living and surviving are two distinct and separate things. Today, I lived. Most days I survive. But, in my current predicament, surviving is better than the alternative.

SO HARD TO DO

Just when I made my determination to finally take my life, I get punched in the testicles.

I was in a really dark place last night. I decided I would end it soon. My plan of a vacation with my love was cemented in my mind. I'd go, have a great time, return home, sink back into the despair and say sayonara. At least, that's what I thought.

I texted my love and told her I was having a bad night. I asked to talk. Sure, it was a temporary high, but I needed it at that moment. I have to drag this out a few weeks until I can hatch my final plan. So, it was necessary.

We talked. I was out of the darkness, but I still was not happy. Then it happened. A few days ago, she took me to a spot that is very near and dear to her heart for the special family memories it represents. It was very cool. It was extremely romantic. We sat on the rocks off a causeway in Miami Beach at 2 a.m. We listened to the waves lap in against the shore. The breeze was just right. We cuddled. We hugged. We kissed. Basically, we just maintained a lot of physical contact. So, it was only right for me to thank her for that experience once again. Her reply crippled me. She said it was a special place to her. She said I was special to her. Now, since she brought me there, that place has even more special meaning to her.

Are you kidding me?

I didn't need that. I really didn't. The main thing keeping me from ending my life is her. I know I will hurt her. I know I will devastate her. But, I also know I will eventually lose her due to my financial situation. It's so hard. Why can't I be rich? Why can't I have success? Why can't I be happy? Why did I have to get hurt, disabled and tossed to the side of society?

The fact that she is so sweet, that she cares so much for me and that she loves me makes this so much more difficult. Somehow, someway, I'm going to have to convince myself that this relationship is a mirage. Surely, when it goes on a few months longer and I still cannot find a way to make money, she'll let me go. I know that will kill me right then and there. And it will just prolong my agony. Why wait? What do I get for delaying things? My reward is just further despair, further hurt, more pain, more self destructive behavior and more time spent as a burden to my friends and loved ones.

As I type this, I realize now what I must do. My vacation plan is materializing. This is what I must do. I'm going the vacation route, taking her away, spending a last few weeks in euphoria. It's the only thing I can do. Go, celebrate life, enjoy it the way it is supposed to be. Then, when I'm back, and the darkness returns, end my life.

That is the best option. I have tried everything else. There are no further plays. I was supposed to write a national magazine, but that fizzled. I was thinking of starting my own magazine, but I was discouraged by those in the industry. I thought I was going to make money through this charity. I was told it could be quite lucrative. Instead, as usual, I got screwed. I haven't heard from the charity director in three days. Another failure. And another potential source of income I told my love that it broke down and amounted to nothing. I can't keep disappointing myself, and I can't keep disappointing her. She deserves better. She deserves more. My love for her is the strongest thing in the world. And, my death will give her some financial relief and allow her to move on to someone who can do what she needs a guy to do for her.

It's just so hard. I want to stay here for her. I want to be here for her. I want to support her, comfort her, love her and cherish her. My situation just won't allow it. We've

already had arguments about me taking up too much of
her time when she needs to work. If she had her way and
didn't have the obligations she did, she would be there
for me as I need her to be. She would work with my
situation. She would accept me for what I am and love
me that way. But her situation prevents that. I know that.
I understand that. I cannot get angry at her. It is simple
economics. Because of my situation, I'm going to lose
her eventually.

So, my decision is final. I'm going to lie to her. I have
to. I swore I would never lie to her, and I meant it when
I said it. Now, unfortunately, there is no other way. I'm
going to tell her I got a bonus from the charity even
though I'll never work a day for it. This way she'll
finally see me as a success. That will make me feel
good, just hearing her say congratulations and seeing her
smile. She'll look at me and think 'My man finally is
doing what I need him to.' I have not had success in
years. I need that feeling one more time. Next, I'll tell
her I hit a few numbers in Powerball. I'll give her some
of the supposed prize. I'll use the rest of the prize to fund
our vacation. She'll go along with it. Happiness will
finally be here for me. Ten glorious days of travel,
companionship, sex and love. Then home to a bottle of
pills, a bottle of alcohol and a few other assorted drugs.
I'll seep away, leaving my carcass behind. The accident,
the fallout, the despair and the situation of my life

already claimed my soul. All that's left is the life in my body, and that will dissipate soon enough.

Clarity. Conclusion. Holy crap. I feel good right now. I'm relieved. I can feel the pain draining from me. I now know what I must do. My decision is made.

I'm doing it.

Once again, good bye.

RUG PULLED OUT

I keep looking for things to keep me here. My love for my family and for the special lady in my life has been pretty much the constant factor to my continued life. I fight for them. I fight because I don't want to know they are hurting from my loss. I fight because I love them, and I fight because it is the proper thing to do.

While I've been caught in this hellhole of a financial situation, there have been several wolves that preyed on me with false hope and grandiose claims.

Two months ago, I reached out to a contact to see if he knew of any freelance positions where I could continue to write about mixed martial arts. He told me his friend was putting out a magazine, and he was looking for someone to write for it.

Perfect. A magazine. Money. Notoriety. A way out. Things couldn't be better. I called the guy. Things looked promising. He wanted me to write a story to prove myself to him. Even though I took offense to that idea, I did it. And, I killed it. The article was awesome.

A few days later, I met Patrick. He didn't really know what was going on with the project. I was giving him idea after idea, and he loved it. But, I don't think he could grasp my vision. He just couldn't get it. He didn't see the big picture.

He was supposed to discuss the national rollout with me the next week. That was more than a month ago. And, I still haven't heard from him.

That hope - followed by the that disappointment - nearly pushed me over the edge. I thought I would be positioned to take care of my love. That made this disappointment even harder to take.

Just when I thought I was over that whole incident, another one came along. My friend George introduced me to a friend of his. Anthony was supposed to start a charity, and there was money to be made through some of the associated business-related items.

Anthony outlined a grand plan, and his marketing company was going to utilize my skills. Finally! I'm saved!

Anthony asked questions about me. He wanted to know why I was so passionate. I explained the situation with my love. It was all for her, I told him. I wanted to make money, provide for her, get her to move up with me and start our new life together. Anthony understood my passion. He understood the situation. He understood how dire it was for me. He looked at me, straight-faced, and reassured me. Everything would be fine, he said. You're going to make money. He told me he would get me a decent sum of money within a month. I believed every word. The depression started to dissipate.

Then he told me the thing I wanted to hear more than anything. Anthony told me to tell my girl to start packing. She was going to be moving up soon. He was that sure of the money I was going to make.

Now, six days later, nothing materialized.

Disappointment and despair returned more than ever before. Holy crap. Things were in my grasp. I was going to have everything I wanted. Anthony reassured me. He knew how important it was. He knew I was dealing with depression and had suicidal thoughts. Yet nothing happened.

What made this disappointment even worse was the idea that I really envisioned my love moving up and living in my house. I was picturing how I would have to move things around to accommodate her and her family. I could almost feel it. It was within my grasp. At least I thought it was. But, nope, another setback. I don't know how many more of these I can take. I had been happy for a few days. Yesterday, I looked longingly at a pill bottle of pain killers. It was simple. It was clear. I wanted to take them. I wanted to go away. I wanted to end it.

But I thought of my love, and I put the bottle down. I walked away.

She saved me again. She's pretty special to have this hold on me while she is 250 miles away. But, that is her gift to me. She gives me life, and I will love her to my dying breath - whenever that is, whether it is in 50 years or 50 seconds. I'm hoping it is years, but with the way I feel, it could be seconds. I won't be doing anything like that tonight, but tomorrow? No promises.

ANOTHER SHOT

Since George is the person who introduced me to Anthony, I wanted to vent to him. George is my Masonic brother. We started together. And we finished together. Before we were to give back our proficiency to conclude our second degree with the Masons, George suffered some emotional trauma. The Masons said if he was not ready by the ceremony, I would move ahead. "Screw that." I remember saying that. I am not leaving him behind. Like I said, we started together and we're ending together.

George got back in time. We engaged in a crash course. I told him to look to me during the ceremony. If he stumbled, I would help. I was his rock then.

He's my rock now.

Since many of the ideas we were going to implement with the charity were the brainchild of George, we decided to start our own organization and move forward. Neither of us will get rich, but there are opportunities to make money with a charity. The charity has to pay for certain things to be performed. We would get those payments. Simple. Easy. Legal. Legitimate.

Finally, I had hope again. I can't do anything now. No way. I see salvation, and it is just a few months away. I can't believe it.

If we can get this thing off the ground, I can make money. Almost as importantly, I can be an inspiration to others by sharing my story. I could speak to groups about the hell I endured. I can tell them how finding love saved me. It's so cliché, but it's so true. Love, truly does conquer all. I was so set on ending my life and eliminating the pain I was constantly in - physically, mentally, emotionally and spiritually. I wanted to end it. I really did. I wanted to die. To be honest, I still do. But, my love for this woman transcends that desire. It makes me want to live. It makes me want to go on. It makes me do anything I can to make some money to help her and get her up here with me. That's my lone focus right now. It's her. It's always her.

I imagine the next few chapters of this journey will be positive. At least, that's how I see them. Who knows though? I could hit a rough patch. I could slip. I could do something stupid. I doubt that will happen, unless this new endeavor crashes and burns. I don't think it will though. We came up with the idea of Operation: Restore Dignity tonight. And we both think it will extend our lives and help us improve our quality of living. Yes, that's right. I said living. If this works, I can live again.

Screw survival. I want to live. And this will help me get there.

Life! Like the Sixx A.M. song, 'Life is beautiful.' Let's hope it is!

MORE ABOUT MY LOVE

I think I need to explain some more about her so you can follow along. You're reading this. You're hopefully getting inspired. I know you've shed a few tears over this manuscript. You had to. If you have a heart, you'll absorb my words and realize the pain and suffering each word contains and how it builds to a crescendo of suffering like few could imagine.

She is perfect to me. She thinks she has flaws. She thinks she is a few pounds overweight. I, personally, love it. I don't want a plastic woman. I want a real woman. And she is very, very real.

Her face is sculpted by angels. I have never had the pleasure of seeing anyone so naturally beautiful. I melt every time I see her. Her smile shines through my soul like a ray of sunshine, and a mere word from her can bring me from the doldrums of my suffering straight to euphoria.

Her personality is amazing. She makes me laugh. She knows what to say. We don't have all that much in common. She is into anime and things of the younger generation. She does not like sports. She does not like many of the movie franchises that are so near and dear to me, things like Star Wars, Star Trek and Lord of the Rings. We do like comedies and horror movies, so at least there is some common ground.

She is bold and adventurous. She encourages me to be the same. I've always been safe. I've always been measured. I never explored the things life had to offer. I was too afraid of stereotypes and labels. I was supposed to be a certain way, and damn it I was going to be that way.

She changes that about me. I've opened up. I've tried new things. And, sexually, she has been a revelation. She got me to come out of my shell. There are things I never thought I would do with any woman. Yet, with her, I crave new experiences. I demand them. I cannot help myself. She wants an adventurous man, someone who could be her equal. I'm determined to be that man. She deserves nothing less than complete and total happiness. I will give it to her.

Yes, she has a child. That is not ideal. It's not that I don't like the kid. I do. I adore him. I would love to help her raise him. And I plan on doing just that. What I meant by 'not ideal' is something different. I want my OWN child. I want to have one with her. I want us to be parents, to share that unique bond that only a mother and father can enjoy. I will be a father to her child. I will provide for him. I will protect him. I will teach him. I will support him. But he will never be my blood, no matter how much I love him and care for him. I'm sure he will say some hateful things as a teenager. Most kids do. My insult will be that I'm not his father. He will be right. But I will not love him a single iota less. He may not be my blood. But he is in my blood. I love that little kid, and I want us to have a great father-son relationship, no matter the difficulties.

My love and I have had just one fight in more than 10 weeks. And, she was right. I know many men say their woman is right to get out of the argument. It's wiser to concede, admit defeat, lick your wounds and go on. But I'm not doing that. She was 100 percent correct. She said she was tired of waiting on me promising things will get done. She wanted action. She needed me to help her. She needed me to help. And it lit a fire under my ass. That's what made the disappointment with Anthony and his lame ass ideas all that much harder to swallow. That was supposed to be my way to make good on what my love wanted.

She explained her position. She cried for 20 minutes as she told me thing after thing. I apologized. I could do no more. Later that night, I said something which she took as a sign I didn't listen to her. She got pissed. She wanted to end it. I explained my position. I did understand. I did listen. I did acknowledge that she was right. But, at the same time, I said what I did because I wanted her to know how much I cared for her. She wanted to spend less time together because she needed to work more. I asked to spend the next night together. I wanted her to know that, despite what she said to me, I was still 100 percent committed to her. Maybe it wasn't wise to ask that right after the argument, but I needed her to know my dedication to her had not wavered. When she finally calmed down and let me explain my position, she understood where I was coming from.

She even agreed to see me the next night. That was the night we went to her special place. And that meant more to me than just about any other honor I've ever had in my life. She brought me to a place where she had such a special memory. To allow me to join in that memory with her proved her love to me. I know she truly loves me now.

I love her more than I can explain. It's funny. I detailed how desperate I felt numerous times. I talked about how I held a gun in my hands, ready to put a bullet through my skull. I explained the desperation, the torment, the pain, the suffering. I found words to describe all those crappy feelings and emotions. Yet, when it comes to explaining how deep my love for this wonderful woman is, I'm speechless. She is the yin to my yang. As Jerry

Maguire found out, this woman truly does complete me. I cannot even fathom what life would be like without her. She is my heart. She is my soul. She is the blood pumping through my veins, bringing life to every inch of my body. She is my other half, and I would rather die than live a moment without her in my life.

I love her. Unconditionally. She is my everything. Thank you for being you. I love you my dear. I LOVE YOU!!!

LAUNCH THE OPERATION

Operation: Restore Dignity is the charity George and I discussed. We are going to work on it in two days. We accomplished so much today. I feel some relief. I feel some optimism. Yes, 'Person of Interest', I feel some hope. Since a person without hope commits suicide, a person with hope decides to live. And, at this moment in time, I have decided to live. I want to live for my love. I want this charity to succeed. I want to help people. I want to inspire people. I want to be there for others to learn from. I want to be there to explain the pain to those who have lost someone to this disease of depression. As Ben said, "Screw off Mr. D. You're not welcome here anymore."

How encouraging it feels right now to speak about life. Yes, life. Not survival, but real life. I feel optimism. I feel hope. It feels wonderful. It feels like a great weight has been lifted off my shoulders.

I have a path with George, and we will succeed. It's too important for us not to. We have to do this. We're going to have to work hard. We're going to have to go in debt. We're going to have to incur some horrific crap. But we'll do it. We have to. George wants me to live, and I said I will. George knows how important my love is to me, and he pledged to do whatever he can to ensure that I am the man she needs me to be. I cannot be anything other than that man. She needs me. I'm willing to do anything in my power to be there for her.

It all starts with a pair of projects. We need to renovate a historic cemetery and a hotel to house homeless veterans. It seems simple. Too simple. But, we'll do it. We'll assist ourselves through legitimate ways. We'll do the work for the charity. We'll give life and hope to others. The charity has already delivered both to me in the past six hours.

POTENTIAL NEW BUSINESS

I attended a medical marijuana seminar over the
weekend. I figured it would be bogus. It was $300 to go.
I shouldn't have gone. I convinced myself it would be a
waste. But, what the hell? My life has been pretty
crappy the past few months. Check that. Pretty crappy
over the past few *years*. Screw it. I paid the admission
and went.

I didn't expect what I saw. I heard that the damn piece of
crap governor of my wonderful state of Florida passed
tough marijuana legislation recently. How tough, I had
no clue. It almost overwhelmed me when the instructors
told us about it. Rick Scott, oh you piece of flotsam, you
passed a medical marijuana bill dubbed 'Charlotte's
Web' to benefit epilepsy patients. It was low-grade
marijuana, with very low levels of THC. That's bad. But,
the fool made it worse.

Scott designated rules that make it nearly impossible to
get into the business. He said an operation would need
to grow, produce and dispense the medication. (As an
aside, medical marijuana is referred to as 'medicine' as
that is truly its purpose.) Scott deemed a nursery would
be required for the grow operation. Not just any old
nursery would do, however. No, this moron said

nurseries must be capable of growing 400,000 plants and trees on its property. It also must be in business continually for the past 30 years. That whittled the list to 39 nurseries across the state. Oh, but that's not all. This maniacal little man said the nursery must have two years of operating costs as liquid assets, which equates to roughly $10 million. On top of that, the nursery must put up a $5 million performance bond. And, of the 39, only five will be chosen to grow the medicine and dispense it. The five will be one in each region of the state - northeast, northwest, central, southeast and southwest.

My marijuana dreams went up in smoke. Literally. But, then a potential brainstorm hit. Christopher Ralph, a brilliant attorney and medical marijuana activist, gave a presentation about the laws. I learned the difference between state law and case law. While marijuana is illegal in Florida via state law, medical marijuana is legal in Florida via case law. Chris showed us how. He also told us about the case of Zvi Baranoff, who created a dispensary for medical marijuana in the Keys back in 1997. The cops caught him, but he got only 18 months probation on a delivery charge. You see, the dispensary itself was not at fault. The circuit court judge ruled Baranoff can use the medical necessity claim for his patients. That gave me the brainstorm.

Perhaps, I could start my own dispensary. Chris showed me how I could get my medical marijuana card, which I applied for earlier today. Once I receive the card, I can grow medication for myself under a case law decision that Chris told us about. And, if I use the Baranoff model, with some revisions, I should be able to open my own dispensary now. Why wait until it passes in November? Let's do the thing now! I asked Chris if he thought this was possible. He said yes. But here's the big thing. Since I would be open before the state issues its next set of guidelines for the other types of medical marijuana, I should be grandfathered in and not have to abide by whatever strict conditions the assholes in Tallahassee decide to screw us over with. Chris agreed with my theory. I set off to create the idea in my head.

I spoke with a friend who works for a large investment bank. I told him the details. I thought he would laugh. Instead, he loved it. We started plotting.

The banker will present the idea to some investors. If it works, he thinks I'm in for a frackin' windfall. A salary of $7,500-10,000 a month sounds nice. So does 50.1-percent ownership of the new company. I immediately said yes. I'm depressed and suicidal. I'm not stupid.

The banker is looking into procuring the money. And he thinks it will fly. Sure, I'm at risk legally, but my life sucks as it is. I wanted to kill myself days ago. Now, I see some hope. Now, I see a future. Now, I see a way to take care of my love, to provide for her and to get her to be with me on a permanent basis. That's all I needed.

I presented the ideas to her. She was nervous at first. But she grudgingly gave it her approval. She wanted to be sure I would be safe. I lied. I said yes. Is that a lie though? I fully believe, 100-percent in my heart, that my plan would ultimately prove legal. I may get arrested. But I would win the legal case, set precedent and tell the state to kiss my rather large backside. Hell, they screwed me with substandard, piss-poor worker's compensation treatment. I might as well get in the final laugh and stick my middle finger in their faces for once.

Hope seems nice. I am smiling. I am listening to music again. And I'm not getting sad when I hear certain lyrics. It's funny. As I write this, I'm hearing 'Life is Beautiful' by Sixx A.M.

"It took a funeral to make me feel alive.
Just open your eyes.
Just open your eyes and see that life is beautiful
Will you swear on your life that no one will cry at my funeral?"

Great song. And it sums up how I feel. Being close to death has revitalized me. It made me feel alive. I see how precious life is. I don't want to commit suicide. I really don't. I want to live. I want to be here to take care of my family. I want to be here to take care of my love. That is important. And, believe it or not, I think marijuana may be my salvation.

It's funny. I covered multiple Super Bowls, the NBA Finals, the World Series, big bowl games, huge MMA fights and a bevy of other important events. But my life may ultimately be remembered as a medical marijuana pioneer. How messed up is that?

It's better my life is surrounded by smoke though. The alternative is my body reduced to ash.

Marijuana, please save me.

MASONIC INTERVENTION

As you can probably sense from reading this manuscript/manifesto/whatever the hell you want to call it, I'm under a lot of pressure.

My family needs me.

My friends rely on me.

My love adores me.

Trying to do right by all of them, especially my love, is hard. I am taking the weight of the world upon my shoulders. It has to work. I cannot disappoint anyone. I'd rather die than do that. And that's not a statement to take lightly. I would literally rather take my damn life than not do what I need to do for my love and for my family. If I fail, well, you read this already. You know the consequence of failure.

Back to my point. Pressure. I went to our regular stated meeting tonight. Prior to the meeting, during our dinner, I had a few Masonic brothers approach me. One asked me if I was ready to show my proficiency at learning a catechism, which is basically a glorified question and answer play. I said I was too busy to really think about that at this time and had way too much on my mind. It was polite, but it was also a please leave me alone kind of message. But, he didn't get it. He then asked if I was ready to go up the chairs, basically go from my officer spot all the way up to lodge president (aka Worshipful Master). Again, I said I had not decided. I don't think he hear me though. He started telling me how he can work with me to get me ready. Sigh. That's two pressure points.

About 10 minutes later, it got worse. The second in command asked to speak with me privately. He asked what my intention was with regard to the chairs. I again answered politely and honestly. I don't know. Well, if I don't want to do the chairs, I could become the secretary. It seems our long-running lodge secretary is having issues with his eyesight, and he wants to step down soon. My name was somehow brought up, and both the number two and secretary thought I would be the ideal replacement. Pressure three. I again said I didn't know. I would think about it. I explained I was in pain. I explained that I was going through severe depression. Did it matter? Nope. I got the speech that it would likely be a three day a week job. Well, unpaid job. Pressure four. I again explained about the depression and said I needed time. Finally, someone relented.

I got hit up again a few minutes later. This weekend, there's a dinner at the lodge to honor our veterans. It's a pork dinner, and I don't eat that crap. I said I may attend, although I'm leaning against it. I have to be there I was told. I need to help them clean up after the dinner. Forget if I have plans on my Saturday night, which I do. It's UFC 173, and I plan on watching it at a sports bar. But that's neither here nor there at the moment. I'm expected to be at the lodge. Pressure five. I'll probably go for 15-20 minutes, say hello, say I cannot stay and bow out of there without eating.

Pressure six wasn't far behind though. After the meeting was over, our number five asked me to write an article about a charitable endeavor we will be doing in a few weeks. Great. More free work. I accepted that one. It will be easy for me. Fifteen minutes and done. Fine.

As we were about to leave, I asked David (our number three) to talk. I called George over. I explained my situation to David. He was very accommodating. He said if I needed to talk, whether it was 1 p.m. or 1 a.m., to just call him. He told me about a personal family loss with a suicide. He supported me. And he told me to tell the people pressuring me to screw off for the time being. It is about healing myself first, mind and spirit. He told me to use the lodge brothers to help myself. They are good, honorable men. Those are the kind of people I need to be around. I would tend to agree, although unless they were each chipping in $25,000, I doubt they can help erase what is truly eating away at my soul.

Still, it was great to have some support. I don't know this guy all that well. Sure, we chat at the lodge, but we haven't spent a single minute together outside of that setting. So it was unexpected to get that kind of reaction from David. I should have expected it though. He's that kind of guy. I appreciated the sentiment, and I know it was real and genuine. Thank you. And thank you for not pressuring me to do anything. Six pressure points were enough already.

NEW MEDICATION

I saw our lodge Worshipful Master, Allan, earlier in the day. I mentioned him previously. I spoke with him about the depression a few weeks ago, and he offered support. He's a doctor who specializes in drug addictions, pain and depression.

I drove 30 minutes to his office in the morning. His wife was the receptionist, and she is a lovely woman. She's very caring, loving, nurturing. I really like her. She was glad I came in, so I can only guess Allan shared my situation with her in some manner. I'm fine with that.

Allan asked me my medical background. We spoke about my pill consumption in previous years. We spoke about the pain levels. We spoke about a variety of things.

Allan's recommendation was a drug called buprenorphine. It is a minor narcotic. But it's long lasting. You put it under your tongue and let it melt away. You absorb it, and it lasts all day once you find your desired dosage.

There are side effects, of course. There are always side effects. Take one pill and it knocks something else off.

Take a second pill for that, but create problem three. It's a vicious cycle, but it's the one our medical system has created.

Allan told me he thinks it would help. I know he truly believes that. He will not lead me astray.

I've just been so inundated with these damn pills over the years that the mere thought of taking more of them instantly got me depressed. I remembered back to the days where I was a member of the Walking Dead cast, meandering from place to place, unaware of my surroundings, searching for food and merely existing as life passed me by.

I don't think I could go back to that. I know I could not go back to that. The mere thought causes me to shudder. I will not be a zombie again. Love the show. Just can't be a cast member like that.

I told Allan I wanted to take some time to think about it. And, I have thought about it. I just cannot allow myself to go down that path. Not again.

I will call Allan sometime next week, tell him I spent days contemplating the offer and politely tell him that I'm declining at the moment. I did just apply for a medical marijuana card, after all. Maybe this drug will help, but I would rather get my medicine naturally. I would rather utilize the medical marijuana to help take away my pain, help restore proper sleep habits and to help me take the edge off my personality so I can finally relax a little bit more. I think that is best for me. Again, who would have thought I would turn to that plant. Who knew marijuana could be so beneficial? I'm discovering that now. It's a wonderful plant that should be celebrated. And, I will give it its proper respect when I eschew other medication and the advice of a dear friend when I chose my medical marijuana over everything else.

THE YO-YO EFFECT

The thing that is most strange about this nightmarish journey that I'm on is the constant up and downs. I jokingly refer to this as a yo-yo effect, as it seems like I'm riding that plastic circle up and down.

As I've thought about this medical marijuana situation over the past two weeks, I've gotten more and more excited. This could get me out of my rut. This could get me on the fast track to money and happiness. Most importantly, this could deliver my love to me, once and for all.

Then I think of her. Again, it's always about her. She is the oxygen to my world. Without her, I'd suffocate and die. Fitting how that phrase is so appropriate here. I cannot live without her. I will not allow it. She is the piece that makes me whole, and she is where my heart truly resides.

While the lady and the money appear on the upswing, meaning my yo-yo should be way up, my emotions generally swing downward as well.

What happens if the weed business fails? The potential profit is huge. Immense. Gargantuan. And, with those projected profits comes the money that will make my life everything I dreamed of. But if it fails? Holy crap. The thought of that plummets my emotions straight to the bottom. I can almost feel the air being sucked from my lungs, my breath shallow, my skin pale and clammy. It feels like the final stages of life, the point where one acknowledges his time is down to minutes, seconds perhaps, and the peace of finality washes over you.

It is that extreme. I know I've said this elsewhere in this manifesto, but it bears repeating again. The highs are the highest feeling you can experience. The lows? They're downright scary at the power and enormity they deliver. They demand your respect. You know you're in the presence of a more powerful entity. Those dark thoughts are mother [expletives]. They call to you. They embrace you. They reassure you. Everything will be alright, they whisper gently into your ear, their hot breath relaxing you, calming you. Yes, this is right you tell yourself. This is the way to go.

But then the happiness shines through, a ray of sunshine on a bleak winter afternoon, piercing the dull, gray clouds and delivering a singular point of expanding light. It grows, eclipses the clouds and starts to brighten the day and mood.

There is no reason to listen to those whispers. Look how brilliant the day is. Accept the warmth. Embrace it. Crave it. Feel the heat warm you. The clamminess evaporates. Things feel normal. Air returns to fill your lungs once again. This is the feeling you want.

Don't listen to those whispers. Listen to the overwhelming way you feel during that warmth, during that high. I keep telling myself this, time and time again. Do not succumb. Be strong. It's almost a mantra worth repeating time and time again. Find that strength. Discover the things life can bring. There is hope. There is optimism. It's time to accept that, welcome that, embrace that. Happiness is truly possible. Give it time. I tell myself all these things numerous times during the day. Much like how often I tell my love how I feel about her, I tell myself these lessons over and over.

Accepting that light and casting away the darkness. It's easy. At least it seems that way. . .

IT'S NOT THAT EASY

When depression sinks its claws into you, it fights to maintain control. It attacks the parts of your mind you didn't even realize were there. It brings shadow. It brings foreboding. Unfortunately, we're not aware enough of this to close shop, once and for all, and tell this feeling to leave us forever.

Instead, we collectively let it in.

As I go through everything I'm going through, several things stand out. It's not easy. It's brave. It's honorable. But, it's difficult as hell.

When you share this type of story with someone who can ask questions, you feel even worse.

"How can you do that to your mother?" They say. "Think what this will do to her. It will devastate her."

Again, it's about them when they say this. They want you to stick around for a guilty reason. They like you. They support you. They need you. They love you.

People claim they understand what you're going through, but how can they? Unless they felt the same pressure I feel, and can feel the same despair as me, how can they know? It's impossible. I know they mean well, but it often annoys me.

It's not easy to put yourself in my shoes. I pray you never have to.

NOW I'M THE ROCK

How did this happen? Somehow, the last few days saw me as the rock for others to rely upon. Two of my friends told me about their problems and situations. They asked me for guidance. They asked me to help them with their depression. I obliged both times and showed my support.

I didn't mind. In fact, I enjoyed it. It showed I may be past this hell that I've found myself submersed in. Did I conquer depression? For a few minutes, I thought I did. Not so fast.

Three days ago, my love calls me. We hadn't had a chance to speak in a few days, and I missed the hell out of her. I answered, all expecting to hear fun and exciting things. Instead, I was exposed to her gloom, and just hearing her sad instantly made me feel the same, like some sort of surrogate sufferer. It was almost like I was trying to will her bad mood onto myself, freeing her to be the angel she is and allowing me to once again wear my comfortable silk-woven rug of doom and gloom.

She was upset about something, but she wouldn't tell me what at first. Finally, it came out. More financial woes. She wasn't making what she wanted. She couldn't pay her mom's internet bill. She was upset.

She said to me at one point that she "wished [she] could lay down, take a nap and never wake up." What? Are you kidding me? It can't be that bad. But, to her, it was.

I instantly sprung to action. I told her that was foolish. Most importantly, I told her that I could not take her loss. If she died, I would follow suit. If she did what I considered for so long, I would take my own life as soon as I learned the news. And I told her so. If she took her life, then she is murdering me, as I will not live without her beautiful soul blessing my life.

She came out of her funk. I offered to pay the internet bill. She finally said okay. We talked about getting together the very next day. Things would be grand. We would finally be together. Life could never get any better.

The next day, she told me she was going out with her family. I later learned our dinner plans were no more. But we did go out that night as promised. We got some drinks. We smoked the hookah and drank kava. We embraced. We kissed. Just seeing her brought me so much joy and elation. But, strangely, it brought great sorrow. Even though I should be enjoying her company, I could not. I knew it was fleeting. I would get a few hours tonight, a few hours later in the week and it was back to being apart. It took an hour for me to finally quell that feeling and simply enjoy her. I love her so much, and I was downright grateful to have her for the short period I received.

We were supposed to spend the night together tonight, but she got pulled away by work. I'd have to wait another night to embrace her fully. I was disappointed. But I understood. This is why I must make money. I need her with me all the time. I have to have her with me. For, without her I would die.

I told her as such. During our date two nights ago, I told her that she saved my life. I don't think she realized that I wanted to take my own life so strongly. It was all I

114

could think about for a few weeks. It still hovers in my thoughts and warms me at night. But, that idea is gone for now, gone because of my love for this beautiful and caring woman. Yes, my love, you truly did save my life this time.

I love you!

THE WRAP UP

This will be my final entry.

No, I have not decided to take my own life at this point. But, I damn well think of it multiple times per day. It's scary at times, yet it is ALWAYS there.

I may do it someday. That day, simply, is not today.

The money situation is still bleak, which is what keeps my mind centered on this. I could not find any investors for the marijuana business. The charitable work with George crapped out. There are a few options on the table with various folks in the adult business world, and I will continue to explore them.

I finally decided to wrap this manuscript and publish it. I think it can help people. I truly, truly do. As I talked about with the entries about Robin Williams and Junior Seau in the preface, people that have not been afflicted by the obsession and thought of suicide never will understand. In some small way, I hope they can read this and find some closure, some small measure to reassure them that their departed loved ones did what they did for justifiable and real reasons. Most of all, I hope people can understand that those who took their own lives were not cowards. They were courageous for themselves, and I respect the decision.

As for me, things with the love of my life remain complicated. She owns my heart, however, and I cannot cause her the pain my actions would create. Yes, taking my own life would be courageous. Living for her is courageous as well. For now, I'm here for her.

I will continue to write my thoughts and continue to seek to motivate others. I have plans on how to market my work, and I truly hope I can touch the lives of as many people as I can.

As I said, for now I've made the decision to stay alive. It could all change tomorrow. That is the curse of this disease. I found my reason to live though. If you're considering taking your own life, I hope you made it through this whole story of mine. If you did, maybe you can find that one thing that makes you stand up and conquer this thing. You're not alone. Talk about this with loved ones. I did. It was embarrassing as all hell. You will feel the same way. Don't go down without a fight. If you ultimately choose to end your life, try to leave something meaningful that will let others know what you felt and why you did it. Touch their lives one final time. Give them the answers to questions they can never ask. That's what this manuscript started out as for me. In a way, it remains as such.

Live. Or die. The choice is yours. Either way, it will take tremendous courage. Hopefully, if you choose the option of death, those left behind will understand your decision through whatever you leave them. And, hopefully, they can accept your decision and celebrate the way you lived rather than the way you died.

The choice belongs to all of us. Be your own hero and make the decision that you have to. I hope you all live, much as I hope I continue to live. But I understand completely if you choose the other option.

Be well. I hope to compile another manuscript in a few years to update you all on my journey through life. I fully plan on it. The 'hope' part comes with the hope of continuing to live. Let's cross our fingers...

2009 GOOD BYE

I originally planned to conclude this manifesto with the note to put a bow on my life. This was to be my last message to the world, the one to be found with my limp and defeated body, the ultimate tribute to the defeat I suffered at the hand of my chronic pain.

I left it open ended and vague so it is applicable to as many loved ones and friends as possible. I felt directing things too finitely would be difficult for whoever I addressed personally.

Here is what I planned as my final message in 2009. I added some to the manifesto to cover the five years since this was first started, but I felt the original final message was important to preserve. Sorry if it is a bit repetitive from the last chapter, but it's important.

I am sure the news of what happened will be considered a shock to many of you.

Right now, there is probably some disbelief, maybe some tears, and definitely some puzzlement.

Allow me to explain what happened. Unfortunately, there is no way to ask any questions, so this will have to serve as the final answer. (I left behind a brief manifesto to further explain my thinking. I can only hope it will one day be published to give everyone a sense of how their actions affect others.)

Many of you know I have suffered from great pain and discomfort in my neck, upper back and arms from an accident years ago. As time passed, the level of pain grew to unmanageable levels. Eventually, my career was impacted. My pain caused me to be bitter and surly, and I was phased out of my company. Nearly two years on worker's compensation did little to cure my ills. The pain level continued to rise.

I sought medical opinion after medical opinion. The doctors in this system are mostly crap. One neurosurgeon saw me for what seemed like 38 seconds. His decision? "Well, 98 percent of people with injuries like yours do not experience the pain you claim to." He dismissed me. And the insurance company took his BS statement and ran with it.

The pain management doctor, supposedly on my side throughout, sold out to the insurance dollars and reversed course on me. The lawyers put the screws to me.

I was faced with the dilemma of returning to some sort of work, despite pain that often resulted in vomiting, or become homeless. Live off the little savings I accumulated, take a laughable settlement and try to survive and eke out a few years worth of an existence.

Put simply, I endured as much pain as one man could tolerate. My body began to shut down at the prospect. I lost my appetite. I lost my mind. And, soon, I lost my will to live. It is a deeply depressing, yet oddly comforting, realization when one decides life is better off at its end. My philosophy when watching loved ones suffer from cancer and other debilitating diseases over the years was to welcome their death and embrace the fact their suffering was finally over. I would be a hypocrite if I did not view my own mortality in that same way.

I began to embrace the release. I knew I was doing what was best for me. Even though I was content with my decision, I struggled for a long time knowing I cause major hurt for those I left behind. Those I loved the most will find this decision crippling, and they will go through immense periods of grief.

To those who feel this way, I implore you to stop crying and listen to me for a minute.

I was suffering. I was miserable. My pain levels crushed me. As a proud person, one with a pain threshold much higher than that of a normal person, I fought as long as I could. Remember, I left the hospital less than five hours after waking up from shoulder surgery and did not take an ounce of pain medication. I did this at a time when most people spend a night in the hospital under heavy dosages of morphine.

That showed me I was not typical. My body did not work like most other people.

When a person such as myself lives with the pain that I did, nothing could save me. It was a matter of time. Rather than suffer any longer, I did the honorable thing. I saved my loved ones from watching the long, drawn out downward spiral, one that assuredly would have resulted in me selling off everything I valued so I could get more and more pills, more and more relief. A life of crime would have ensued. I would have passed as a broken and pitiful man.

Instead, I left with my head held high. I know I fought the good fight for as long as I could. Do not pity me or cry for me. Embrace me and the lessons learned from me.

Know that my suffering has finally come to an end. Know that I finally can rest without pain. Know that I finally can know an existence where pain does not define me. I embraced the end of my long-standing battle with pain. Celebrate that. Celebrate my release. Do not grieve my passing. I know it will be difficult for many to accept. But, please, honor my memory and feel good knowing my suffering finally, and humanely, came to an end.

I love all of you, and I hope there is an afterlife so we can all be reunited again in a blissful and pain free existence. I hope to see you all again soon.

Until then, fight the good fight as long as you can. I love you and will miss you, but my time has come.

Good bye.

NEW ENDING

I didn't think I could close this book with my written words. Instead, I figured I would be dead, the final chapter never written, the final deed left undescribed. Oh, I planned on saying how I intended to take my life and what my method would be. But, I knew people would never know if I did it or not, so I figured I would become an interesting Google search.

What I didn't think would appear is an actually happy ending.

No, my love and I have not resolved things, and we remain geographically apart. My marijuana business never launched off the ground. Money is not coming in. Yes, I'm surviving, but I see the hope for the future.

And, that my friends, is the important lesson in this whole storm I've laid out for you. I was at desperation levels. I wanted to take my own life. I fantasized about it. I obsessed over it. I wanted it, and damn it I was going to have it.

But something funny happened. I lived just long enough to get over the feeling. I was able to see the possibility that things were going in my direction. I had hope of life once again, and it was wonderful.

That lesson is what needs to be absorbed out of this book. Just when you think despair will overtake you, fight for that extra day. I did. I thought of my love, my feelings for her, how much I would hurt her. I thought of that beautiful face contorted in agony, tears full of mascara dripping down her face, engraving lines like the Grand Canyon onto that flawless skin. No. I could not allow myself to do it. I found my reason to live. My reason was my love, and she will always be special to me as long as I still breathe.

Now, if you're in the place that I was for much of this story, you know I'm speaking directly to you. I fought the urge. I battled. I clawed my way out. I somehow found something that worked for me. I still can't believe it. But, I did.

If you're in that type of shape, follow my advice. Fight that feeling. Don't give in.

But, if he is going to win, find a way to bless one or two of your loved ones. Make a difference. Let your death bring some good to others.

It takes strength and courage to pursue either option. If you fight it and somehow win, try to write ne with some personal reflections. Tell me what made you win. And, if you are going to succumb to this, write me before you do it. Tell me how you felt, what you experienced, how you found the courage to do it.

I am not telling you to save your life, nor am I telling you to take it.

That is a deeply personal situation that only you can decide. It is your choice. Know that both paths will be easy. You're now screwed. You're in a battle. Will the battle to move on and continue to fight be your objective? Or will it be to simply find peace and end your suffering. Choose wisely,

I know I made that choice in the past few days. I don't know how I made it, but somehow I did. I chose to live on, to fight, to struggle and to hope. I chose that. I chose life. Unfortunately, the other choice is the only one permanent. You can't come back from that one, say oops, and move on.

But, if you chose life today, you can fight. And if you choose death today, you have my adoration and respect. You made the choice I know I should have. That was the best option. I chickened out.

But there is still the chance. And, with that chance comes more topics to write about.

Hopefully I stay on my path and continue to live long enough for you to read Volumes 2 and 3.

Stay tuned. And, if you don't see that new volume, Google me to get closure to my life's story.

Thank you so much for reading this, and thank you for allowing me to give you insight into what made my decision to take my own life so difficult. Learn from my words. Absorb them. Take solace in them.

If you lost someone to suicide, realize how brave that person was, how difficult the choice was to them. If you are thinking about suicide, know you're bit alone. Hope my words bring you clarity and comfort. If you're reading this to learn, I hope you gathered helpful knowledge. And, finally, if you're reading this because you're a loved one and I took my own life, I hope you understood how much I hurt, how painful it was to leave you and how much I love you.

Take from this what you will.

I love you.

Finally: My love, you are my world. Thank you. I love you most of all. I hope I become the man you need me to be.

DEDICATION

This was originally penned in 2009.

This work was created during a period where I contemplated suicide for multiple reasons that will be documented over the remaining pages.

Whether or not I go through with the act is inconsequential. These thoughts were formulated during my darkest and most vulnerable time.

This manifesto is dedicated to those I will ultimately leave behind. My loved ones must know what I was thinking. This was written so they could understand me and my decisions.

This was also written to give the world a glance into a very private and desperate time in a person's life. My hope is that my words will inspire change – politically, legally and medically. My hope is that no one else suffers my fate due to the corrupt system we are all governed by. Let my words serve as a warning and an inspiration for change and reform. Let others who are going through the same situations as I did find strength in my words, and let them find solutions I was too weak to find on my own.

I hope I leave this world a better place and inspire others with my words. If I do that, it was all worth it. My life was a success.

To my parents and brother, I hope you forgive me for what I believe I will do. You have been the rocks of my life, and you have been loved and appreciated. I will miss you the most.

To my closest friends, I thank you for your friendship. You all became like brothers to me. Your love, support and guidance were integral to the success of my life. To Jose, you passed before me, and I have missed you ever since.

Added in 2014:

To my love, you never knew or understood how much I loved you. Now, you finally know. Thank you for blessing my life and giving it some meaning once again. I hope to grow old with you. I love you in this world and through eternity. U KICW TIY, I LOVE YOU.

ABOUT THE AUTHOR

 Bob Emanuel Jr. was born to parents Bob and Martha Emanuel on Dec. 26, 1974. His brother, Chris, was born the next year and suffered from a mental handicap.

Bob attended McArthur High School in Hollywood, Florida, before he landed a scholarship to the University of Miami. There, he switched majors from pre-medicine to journalism. After his second year at the school, Bob transferred to Florida International University, from where he graduated in 1996.

Bob gained employment at the Miami Herald in Sept. of 1996 and worked his way from a freelancer to a reporter during his career, which ran until Sept. of 2008.

Bob's injuries were sustained as a passenger on a trip to Orlando to cover the XFL for the Miami Herald on Feb. 3, 2001, when the vehicle he was in was struck by another motorist. Bob continued to work at the Miami Herald until he was laid off in 2008.

After Bob went on Social Security Disability in 2010, he wrote and maintained a nationally syndicated column on mixed martial arts for the Scripps Howard News Service. As part of his position, Bob participated in the Ultimate Fighting Championship's fighter rankings, a great source of pride.

Bob joined the Masonic order in 2013 and was risen to Master Mason within seven months. He was appointed an officer of the Groveland lodge for 2014.

Bob maintained his residence in Hollywood throughout his life before he moved to Clermont in 2013.

www.ingramcontent.com/pod-product-compliance
Lightning Source LLC
Chambersburg PA
CBHW070357290526
45790CB00004B/1526